I love Brazil
travel guide

By S. L. Giger as *SwissMiss on Tour*

"Don't count the days. Make the days count."
- Muhammad Ali

Receive a free packing list

Never forget anything important ever again and don't waste unnecessary time with packing. Send an e-mail with the subject: **packing list** and receive a free packing list along with a sample of my Thailand travel guide.

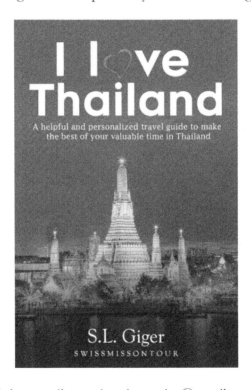

Send the e-mail to swissmissstories@gmail.com and receive your free gift.

Content

Why should I choose this guidebook instead of any other?

Do you only have a limited amount of time (like two or three weeks) and feel a bit overwhelmed by the huge size of the country? Where should you start? How can you select the places to visit if there are so many highlights to be seen in Brazil? This guidebook will help you to really focus on the must-sees of Brazil. Better don't forget your camera and be ready to take in incredible views.

Probably, the usual guidebook which talks about every small city will burst your timeframe. Therefore, you only find the best of the best in I love Brazil, which still could easily fill three weeks to a month, but you can also visit it in less time.

Do you want to plan your own, smooth journey in Brazil? This guidebook will help you to do just that.

Before my first Brazil trip, I worried about the people not speaking English and about safety in general. I thought I would get robbed, held at gunpoint and surely be an easy target as a solo female traveler. Yet, some people I knew had just been to Brazil and were completely raving about their experience – while also saying that you need to behave according to the local safety rules. So, I included a list of safety advice for traveling in Brazil. With this help, I traveled on public buses and went out for dinner or to dance after dark – and was completely fine. Every day, the beauty of Brazil blew me away! I liked it so much, that I went back a second time, to see more of the country.

As a European, it's hard to get a grasp on the size of Brazil. I still haven't seen everything I want, and I'll hopefully come back soon but for now, it's your turn to experience the beauty, the colors, and the vividness.

If you read this guidebook, you will get to experience the best of of Brazil without having to do any further research. You find a two-week travel itinerary with detailed "how to"-guidelines and further ideas and descriptions.

In case you are worried about the Portuguese language, there is a small language guide with helpful words at the end of this book. Otherwise, you should be fine with hands, feet, and in seldom cases, Google translate.

So, what are you waiting for? Have fun exploring!

Reasons to look forward to your journey in Brazil in case you are not entirely convinced yet

Perhaps you are a bit worried about safety if it is your first trip to Brazil. However, Brazil has amazing places that need to be discovered. Colorful murals and houses wherever you go. Modern cities with great art museums, incredible beaches for surfing as well as simply to enjoy. You don't like water? Well, what about heading to a stunning desert? Or a green canyon? Perhaps, you'd rather join a samba party? A must visit is the biggest and very beautiful Iguazu Waterfall. You can even head across to Argentina for one day.

I don't speak Portuguese and although not many people speak English, it was always easy to find the information I needed as the people are friendly and will help you.

In the end, Brazil wasn't any different regarding safety than any other country in South America that I have visited. Read the section about **safety advice** in this travel guide and I'm sure you will have such a great time in Brazil as I did.

About the author of this guidebook

Seraina loves to travel since she can remember. It started with beach vacations with her family when she was a child but soon, she sought her own routes. She was lucky to be able to spend an amazing High School year in New York at 15 years old. That's when she started to write her first travel blog which evolved into SwissMissOnTour (http://www.swissmissontour.com/). Later, she explored

Europe with Interrail but was also attracted by the exotic countries further away. Countless trips to South East Asia made her fall in love with the delicious Asian flavors, beautiful temples and nature highlights. South America was always at the back of her mind but for that, she wanted to have more time in order not to have to fly back and forth to Switzerland in every vacation. So, when the timing was right, she quit her job and is now fully enjoying the countries of South America. As she was writing this, she was sitting on a rooftop terrace in Lima, still enjoying every minute of this great journey.

Brazil Highlights

In a country which is as large as Brazil, it's hard to pick what is best. There simply are so many diverse and incredible places. But here are my three highlights.

1 Iguazu Falls

Be impressed by the massive wall of water and the sound of this beautiful waterfall.

2 Bay of Rio

This city has probably the most beautiful bay in the world.

3 Chapada Diamantina - Pai Ignacio

You thought that the Grand Canyon is a unique spectacle of nature? Then, you have to come to Chapada Diamantina, and you will believe that you traveled back into a time of dinosaurs.

Things to consider before you visit Brazil to have the best possible trip

In this chapter, you find all the information you need to know for a smooth journey in Brazil.

Currency

Brazil uses Brazilian Reais/Real. The short form is R$ or BRL. At the moment of writing this book, 1 USD equals 4 BRL. To have the correct conversion during your trip, use Google and search for USD to BRL.

In most restaurants, shops, and hostels you can pay by credit card without a surcharge. Only for things you buy from street vendors or if you board a public bus you will need cash.

Visa and Vaccinations

No visa is required for Brazil if you want to stay up to 90 days. You only need a valid passport with an empty page for the entry stamp. The passport needs to be valid for 6 months after entering Brazil.

Since there is an increase in yellow fever cases in Brazil the WHO recommends having a yellow fever vaccination. However, it's not mandatory.

Also, there is a high rate of dengue fever cases. Unfortunately, there is no vaccination against dengue. Therefore, wear long clothes when mosquitos are around and use an anti-mosquito spray with a high DEET factor.

To avert mosquitos, locals gave me the following tip (I haven't tried it but so many people have sworn that this works): Every morning you should put 40 drops of Propolis (Propoleo) in half a cup of water and drink it. Start with this treatment 5 days before you go to a mosquito-infested area.

If you spend a longer amount of time in the Amazon, it's recommended to have an anti-rabies vaccination.

Drinking water

The tap water in Brazil is not drinkable and you could suffer from severe stomach infects if you drink tap water. Therefore, even with ice cubes, you should always ask whether they are made of filtered water. I went so far that I even brushed my teeth with filtered water. Luckily, this way, I had no health problems.
Sometimes, there are water dispensers in the accommodations, where you can fill up your bottles free of charge. Often, this was a clay filter and the water had a slightly earthy taste. Apart from that, however, this naturally filtered water was germ-free! If, in addition to the faucet, there is a smaller faucet on which you can divert the water by turning a lever, this is the pipe for filtered water. So, I would have rarely had to buy filtered water in Brazil. However, I didn't have to buy any water at all, because, as usual in South America, I had my travel water filter with me.

I use the red and white drinking cylinder from **DrinkPure**. Great about this product is that it comes from a Swiss

quality brand. My health is important to me and I don't want to take any risks with something as basic as drinking water. DrinkPure states that both 99 % of bacteria and 99 % of viruses are filtered, which is not the case with other travel water filters. That's why I like to accept the somewhat bothersome filtering process by pushing water from one bottle to another. I need about 10 minutes per liter of water. Consequently, you can avoid plastic waste, save money and certainly always have drinking water, even if you arrive at a new place in the middle of the night and the shops are already closed.

The **DrinkPure** water filter is best suited if you take it on a hike and screw it directly onto the drinking bottle. Then you can immediately drink as much as you desire.
You can buy the DrinkPure filter here:
https://www.drinkpure-waterfilter.com/water_filter/.

1.
FILL YOUR
BOTTLE

2.
SCREW
ON

3.
SQUEEZE,
DRINK,
ENJOY!

How to stay safe in Brazil

I only once felt slightly unsafe in Brazil while walking down a deserted alley in Salvador during the day. So, 99% of my stay I spent worry-free. However, I did hear firsthand stories of other people (also locals) who were robbed (with and without guns). I listened to their tips on how to avoid such incidents, and since I had a good experience while following them, I hope you can also enjoy a carefree time in Brazil if you follow these 7 points.

- **Ask the locals about safety advice**

Locals know best how safe a certain place is. So, ask your hotel or hostel if you can hike to that secret beach by yourself or if it's okay to take a public bus to a certain place. I contacted all my hostels beforehand if it was safe to reach them by public transport or whether I should take a taxi. So, on my fifth night in Brazil, I found myself walking to my hostel from the bus station after dark with all my belongings in Chapada Diamantina. The alleys got smaller and steeper, there were just a few dogs, cats, and no people, and it wasn't even a paved road anymore. Not a place I would choose for a stroll in Switzerland during the night. Yet, the hostel told me it was safe, and actually, that was just the normal way to get to the hostel since Lençois is a charming, small-town far away from bigger cities. Tourism is giving everybody jobs with a good income and consequently, there is a 0-crime rate in Lençois right now. But situations can change and therefore, it's always good to ask the locals. You can use Google Translate to translate

16

your questions into Portuguese or just see if they speak English.

- **Stay in populated areas**

It's more likely that an armed robbery will happen if you are the only person in an alley. Therefore, try to explore the parts of the town where other people are out and about as well. On the other hand, if you are in very crowded areas such as Copacabana or Ipanema beach or anywhere during a carnival festival, just don't bring any valuables or never put them out of your hands. At the beaches of Rio, backpacks get stolen from under the feet of tourists every day. There, you need to be extra careful.

- **Don't wear jewelry**

Perhaps, I overdid this a little, but better safe than sorry. I left my finger ring at home and didn't wear my watch, earrings nor any bracelets or necklaces.
A girl who worked as a volunteer in Sao Paolo told me that they ripped a rock pendant from her neck. It wasn't anything expensive as she had bought it as a souvenir in Colombia but still, she got robbed. Hence, better not wear anything at all.

- **Leave your phone in the hostel locker if you don't absolutely need it**

I took pictures with my phone in all the cities although other travel guides don't recommend walking around with your phone on the streets. Yet, all the locals do it as well.

Hence, it's a risk as people do get robbed but it's not like people will steal your phone as soon as you snap a picture. The more you are alert while using your phone, the less it will get stolen. What is dangerous is when you get from A to B in the night or are in very crowded places and keep your phone in your pocket or bag. If you can avoid it, don't bring your phone when you go out in the evening or when you go to the beach. Locals recommend having a second, cheap phone which they bring with them and can hand over in case they get robbed. However, all the tourists I met who got their phone stolen were either drunk or sleeping at that time.

- **Use Uber**

The bigger cities all have Uber. The taxis are trackable which makes them safer. While I used the bus and metro in Sao Paolo and Rio both during the day and during the night, it's not always advisable to walk from the hostel to the bus station or any other short distances. Better order an Uber or let someone else order one for you, in case you didn't bring the phone.

- **Spread your money**

Don't keep all your cards and money in one wallet. Spread them across several places of your luggage. Only always bring as much money as you think you will need for the time you will spend out of the hostel. In Brazil, it is very common to buy everything with a credit card. Hence, you don't necessarily need to walk around with cash. However, then, a robber could take a detour via an ATM with you.

Such robberies have happened, but I haven't heard a firsthand account from one. Yet, several people told me that a robber with a knife or gun demanded their cash and phones. For those cases, better always keep a fake wallet with a small amount of money with you and just hand it over to the robber in case you do get robbed.

- **Walk around with a plastic bag or cheap shopping bag**

Instead of an expensive-looking purse or camera bag, just bring your camera or anything else you carry with you in a cheap plastic bag. I traveled through South America with a free, reusable shopping bag and sometimes carried my laptop around in it while nobody would have expected that. Make yourself look like you have nothing worth robbing.

So, with those tips, I hope you will only experience the positive sides of Brazil.

How to have a good experience on Brazilian buses

If you travel around Brazil by bus you might have several trips of 7 hours and longer ahead of you. They can be enjoyable if you read the following tips.

How to book a ticket

The cheapest option is to book directly with the bus companies at the bus station. To check times and bus companies, you can go on www.busbud.com/en /country/br. You can book on their website as well but there is a surcharge fee.

You will need to show your passport along with your ticket, so keep your passport on you. Sometimes, you have to show the ticket several times and therefore, don't throw it away until you reach your destination. Especially on short day buses.

How to keep warm on the night bus

Night buses in Brazil are freezing! I am not kidding about that. I was wearing a hoodie, my down jacket, and my rain jacket. The rain jacket was great to block out the air from the a/c. Of course, also long pants and socks. With all those layers, I was fine and even managed to sleep.

How to stay safe on the bus

I didn't have any problems regarding safety on my bus rides. I always check my big backpack in the compartment below the bus. In that bag, I have my laptop, one of my two credit cards and part of my money. If the bus gets robbed, it's usually on the bus by people who come and leave during stops. Therefore, keep anything you take on the bus on your body. The best is if you have an invisible hip belt for your passport, some money, and your phone. Or if you have a pocket with a zipper on your jacket, you can also put the phone in there, while keeping your hand on the pocket. Several phones of other people got stolen while people were sleeping, and they woke up with just their headphone cord in their open pocket. Also, the hand luggage of other people got stolen out of the overhead compartment or from below their seat. Never put your backpack in the upper baggage compartment, even if a supposed bus employee wants to help you store your luggage up there. This, too, is a tactic to steal valuables. Another possibility is that the person sitting behind you can rob you by reaching below the seat. The safest way is to have only clothes, food and water in your hand luggage and to keep this between your legs.

Wi-Fi

All of our accommodations offered free Wi-Fi. Further, there is free Wi-Fi at Starbucks, most restaurants, and in many public places in the bigger cities. Hence, you don't necessarily need to have data. However, to be able to order an Uber from any location in a city, a data package is useful. Unfortunately, Brazil has been the most complicated country so far to get a local sim card. Most people I met needed a whole day in phone shops until they finally had a working sim card with internet. In case you don't want to waste a day of your vacation but still need data, it might be better to check data plans for abroad with your own phone provider from home. I bought a small package from Switzerland and didn't even use it up since I mostly could access free Wi-Fi.

Finding your way

As everywhere I go, I used the **maps.me** app on my phone and downloaded Brazil for offline use. This has been a very useful companion every day and always brought me to the place I wanted to go. You can use it to find points of interest within the city, to get to your accommodation or to follow a hiking route. Tourists can mark spots and write comments and hence you can even discover secret spots which other tourists recommend.

Brazilian food and drinks you need to try

Okay, I have to say that I wasn't too excited about lots of the local dishes. I am a foodie and love to eat delicious creations with many flavors, whether they are salty, spicy or sweet. However, in Brazil, many dishes just are greasy and feel heavy. For breakfast, they often serve cake. Which, usually, I would be thrilled about, except that the cakes did not live up to my taste buds. Then, you don't really want to start your day with an unhealthy calorie bomb.

However, I did find a few awesome delicacies, which you need to try.

- **Tapioca**

This is kind of a crepe or taco made of yucca flour. I generally love the yucca root and tapiocas are an awesome product created with the starch inside the flour. You often find people selling tapiocas from small street carts or on breakfast menus. They simply heat the flour in a pan, and it starts sticking together. Then, you chose a filling like chicken, cheese or tomato. It can also be sweet (banana or Nutella). My favorite was with cheese, arugula, and sun-dried tomatoes.

- **Fruit**

Brazil has so many fruits with exotic names and tastes that I still don't know which one is which. It's worth tasting yourself through all the fruits you encounter. Many taste as sweet as candy. Plus, most of them need to be peeled or opened up and hence are safe to eat for your stomach (general anti-diarrhea rule: peel it, cook it or leave it).

- **Caipirinha**

This is Brazil's refreshing national cocktail made of cachaça, lime, and sugar. You can find them anywhere and prices start as cheap as 7 BRL. In addition, you can have them with fruity flavors like strawberry, maracuja and much more.

- **Caipiroskas**

Many Brazilians actually prefer this to Caipirinha. Here, the cachaça is substituted by vodka. Try both and decide which one you like better.

- **Burgers**

No matter where you eat a burger in Brazil it will be absolutely delicious. It might not be healthy, but they sure know how to prepare a juicy burger that is full of flavor. Whether it's a cheap burger from a street cart or one in a restaurant, you can't go wrong.

- **Moqueca**

This is a fish stew with coconut milk, garlic, bell peppers, onions, tomatoes, and cilantro. It's delicious and filling. Often, the pan is meant to be shared by two people.

- **Parrillas**

My mouth already starts watering if I only think about it. Parrillas are meat restaurants where they gill meat to perfection. Often, you pay for a buffet and they walk up to your table serving you fresh cuts of the meat of your choice. If you want to treat yourself to a buffet with really good quality, try **Fogo do Chao** (www.fogodechao.com/). There are several restaurants with this name (for example in Sao Paulo and Rio). Go hungry, as you probably want to try everything.

- **Cheap lunch menus**

Like most countries in South America, Brazil also has its version of good value lunch menus. Sometimes they also have them for dinner. They are marked as "PF". Ask the restaurant if they have a PF if there is no sign outside.

Brazilian customs

Soccer

Soccer is pretty much holy in Brazil and much of the country is following the matches. You will notice when a game is on as people gather in bars and restaurants to have a beer and watch the game. So, it's a much more social activity than what I am used to in Switzerland as people don't seem to watch the games alone in their living room but anywhere where there is a tv in public. They are happy if you join one of their tables to watch the game with them.

Carnival

Carnival in Brazil is so popular that the pictures of women in feathery dresses who dance to Samba music are enough to attract visitors from all over the world to watch this spectacle. The most famous Carnival takes place in Rio de Janeiro but almost every city has its own festivities.

Carnival takes place between the Friday afternoon before Ash Wednesday and Ash Wednesday at noon (usually in February). So, it's a Christian holiday to celebrate the time before the lent which leads up to Easter. The word Carnival comes from "carnelevare" which means "to remove meat".

The parades are organized by Samba schools and are a colorful event to watch.

If you want to visit Brazil during Carnival, be sure to book your accommodation at least 6 months, if not a year ahead as you are not the only one who wants to be there for the festival. Plus, be extra careful when you are out and about. It's an easy playground for pickpockets. Hold on to your phone or camera the whole time! Don't get wasted or you will most likely get robbed.

Tips how to find cheap flights to Brazil (and to any other country for that matter)

Lucky me, the cheapest flights from Switzerland to South America often are to Sao Paulo. In order that you can also find a good flight deal for yourself, try booking with the following tips.

1 Use several flight search engines

I usually start looking for flights on Skyscanner (https://www.skyscanner.net/) and then I compare the deals from there with **CheapTickets** and/or **Opodo**. These sites tend to have the cheapest prices. Skyscanner for example, lets you set a price alert which will inform you with an e-mail when they have cheaper flights. You could do that half a year before your trip. Another possibility is to type your flight into Google directly to get an estimate of how much the airfare will be. In the end, I always check on the websites of my favorite airlines directly. For South America, they are Swiss and Latam.

2 Be early and buy your flight at least 3 months ahead

If you know the dates of your vacation, there is no use to wait with booking your flights. They will only get more expensive. However, if you are very flexible with your plans, check Urlaubsguru (https://www.urlaubsguru.de/) for cheap last-minute deals and other travel deals (although last-minute plane tickets usually are a lot more expensive than when you book early).

3 Be slightly flexible

Check the dates three days prior and after the dates you chose to fly. There might be a difference up to $300! If you search with Cheaptickets or Skyscanner it's very easy to have an overview of the flight prices at different dates.

4 Travel from other airports and book multi-leg flights

Especially if you travel from Europe it makes sense to check the airports in the surrounding countries and then buying a connecting flight from your country to get there. Cheaper airports to fly from are Barcelona, London, Frankfurt am Main, Düsseldorf, Paris, Milan, Amsterdam, and Brussels. So, yes, if you have enough time, it's sometimes worth it to travel in several legs. If you fly from the US, often Miami and LAX are the cheapest. Just calculate enough time in your connecting airport in case your first plane is delayed because you will have to go get your luggage and check it in for your new flight.

5 Delete your browser history

The websites where you checked for your flight tickets to Brazil will recognize you on your second visit and raise the prices a little since you are still interested. So, if you notice an increase in the price, the first thing to do is to close the website, clear the browser history and then start searching again, once you are ready to book.

6 Sign up for the newsletter from your favorite airlines

Newsletters still offer good value and often you find cheap airfares in them. At the moment, I regularly receive special offers from Tui and Iberia. By the way, SwissMissOnTour offers a newsletter as well.

Sign up on www.swissmissontour.com to receive my latest blog posts and a free and helpful packing list.

7 Flying cheap within Brazil

If you book the flights several weeks ahead, you can find flights within the country which are cheaper than the bus rides. Therefore, it's worth it to plan your trip ahead. I flew with the low-cost airline GOL (www.voegol.com.br/pt) and was satisfied with all the flights. It's cheapest to book directly on their website and with Portuguese set as the language.

Two-week itinerary to see the best of culture and nature

I have to tell you right now that two weeks won't be enough time to see all the wonders of Brazil. To see most of the highlights, I created a very dense itinerary for you (see below). However, if you don't feel like squeezing so much into such a short time, it's better to cut something and return to Brazil another time.

Day 1: Fly to Foz do Iguacu

Get an international flight to Sao Paulo and then a connecting flight from there to Foz do Iguacu. Take it easy on the first day and find a good place to eat.

Day 2: Iguazu in Argentina

Today, you are actually already leaving Brazil for one day to visit the stunning side of Iguazu waterfall in Argentina. Be wowed by the power of the water. Return to Foz in the evening.

Day 3: Iguazu in Brazil

Of course, you also want to see this incredible waterfall from the Brazilian side. You won't need the whole day for it. Hence, you could visit another attraction in the afternoon or take a flight to Salvador in the late afternoon or evening. Otherwise, you will fly to Salvador very early the next morning.

Day 4: Salvador and night bus Lençóis

Visit the colorful old town of Salvador and marvel at the houses. Then, relax by a beach or ride the Lacerda elevator to the lower section of Salvador. In the evening, take a night bus to Lençois.

Day 5: Lençóis

Relax after your night bus and visit the sights close by like the rock pools or a waterfall. Book a tour of Chapada for the next day.

Day 6: A tour in Chapada Diamantina

Your tour will bring you to see all the highlights of Chapada. It's a long day filled with amazing places.

If you are well organized, you then can take a night bus back to Salvador directly after your tour and fly to Rio from Salvador the next morning. Then, you have some more time in Rio. However, you might not feel like another night on a bus and perhaps you want to let the experience settle a little. Therefore, spend another night in Lençóis.

Day 7: Transfer to Rio

Take an early bus to Lençóis. This will take 7 hours and be quite uneventful. In Salvador, take a bus or Uber to the airport and get an evening flight to Rio. If you have the necessary cash, you could also fly from Lençóis to Rio.

Day 8: Rio de Janeiro

Take a walk through the historic center and later relax at one of the famous beaches like Copacabana or Ipanema. You will feel the vivid spirit of this city all day.

Day 9: Rio de Janeiro

Visit some museums and stroll along Flamengo walk. Return to the beach again in the late afternoon.

Day 10: Ilha Grande

Take an early bus to Conceição de Jacareí and from there, take the boat to Ilha Grande. Relax at the beaches near your hostel.

Day 11: Beach time

Take a boat to Playa Lopez Mendes and spend some time at one of the most beautiful beaches in Brazil. Spend another night on Ilha Grande.

Day 12: Sao Paulo

Take the first boat to Angra dos Reis and then catch a bus to Sao Paulo. The bus ride takes 7 to 8 hours. Hence, you will only arrive in Sampa in the evening. However, you will catch some nice views of the coast along the way which will make you want to return to Brazil and spend some more time along the beaches between Rio and Sao Paulo.

Day 13: Sao Paulo

Today you have a full day to explore this huge city. Of course, one day is not enough, especially for such a big metropolis but you could start by looking at the graffiti in Vila Madalena. Later, you take the metro to the central market and taste yourself through the fruits and have a delicious lunch. After that, you could walk toward the cathedral of Sé and get a short glimpse of the center of Sampa. You end the day along Paulista Avenue.

Day 14: Sao Paulo and return flight

Hopefully, your return flight is in the evening, that you have one more day to eat in a parrilla house and see more of Sao Paulo.

Another itinerary option:

If you cut out Salvador and Chapada Diamantina and fly directly to Rio instead, you need one less flight and have some more days which you could spend in Paraty, Rio, and Sao Paulo.
Then, your tour would be a nice triangle.

Now, we first have a more detailed look at the individual places.

Iguazu Waterfall

Iguazu waterfall is one of the 7 wonders of the world and really merits this title. It's a huge waterfall which consists of hundreds of individual waterfalls. If you are a waterfall lover, Iguazu is a must but even if you don't care too much about waterfalls, Iguazu will impress you.

The question which many people ask themselves is which side of the waterfall to visit. The Brazilian or the Argentinian one? I ask, why choose? You will travel a long way to come here and it would be a shame not to appreciate the waterfall from all its angles. I explain you how to visit Iguazu in Brazil and you will also find out how to visit Iguazu in Argentina.

How to visit the Brazilian Falls from Foz do Iguacu

The town closest to the Brazilian Iguazu is called Foz do Iguacu. You can get here by traveling by bus for several days from Sao Paolo or the southern beaches. However, if you look up to two weeks before your trip, you will find flights from the bigger cities in Brazil that will end up cheaper or only slightly more expensive than the long bus rides in Brazil. GOL has the cheapest prices and it's best to book on their website in Portuguese.

From Foz do Iguacu airport to the city center

The airport you will land near the Iguazu Falls is called Foz do Iguacu (IGU). To get into town from the airport you can take Uber, a taxi or bus number 120 (3.75 BRL). The bus leaves every 20 minutes and the bus driver will give you change up to 20 BRL. Use *maps.me* to spot your hotel and get off at the closest bus station. Just be sure to take the bus that goes downtown (it takes about 30 minutes to the main terminal). Because the same bus also drives to the Brazilian side of the waterfall in the opposite direction.

Where to stay in Foz do Iguacu

I stayed at CHL Suites near the main bus terminal. This was a good choice as it was clean, and they offered free Caipirinhas in the evenings. Also, Foz felt safe and it was easy to walk to the many nearby restaurants and the supermarket.

How to get to the Brazilian side of the waterfall from Foz

So, as you already know, you can take bus 120 for 3.75 BRL. It takes 35 minutes from the main bus station. Which means, Foz airport is 5 minutes from the falls. You could also go to the falls directly from the airport. There are lockers that fit 50 L backpacks.

Visiting the Brazilian side of Iguazu Falls

The entrance fee is 70 or 80 BRL and can be paid by credit card or cash. You can also pre-book the ticket online on cataratasdoiguacu.com.br. Once you have your ticket, you get in line to board a double-decker bus. This will bring you to the first viewing platform. If you booked an additional boat ride or some other excursion at the entrance, you might have to get off at another stop before that. An audiotape on the bus lets you know.

The first platform already gives you an impressive front view of a big part of the waterfall.

After that, you leisurely walk along the path for about an hour with many good photo opportunities along the way. In the end, you reach a boardwalk that leads below the falls. Probably, you need a raincoat, or you will be soaked. You can buy ponchos there but as the prices are very touristy, it's better if you bring them from home.

From there you can either take an elevator or walk up the stairs past several other platforms to reach a restaurant and the food court. Then, take a double-decker bus back to the entrance.

So, with taking it slowly you need about 2-3 hours for your visit.

Even though there are fewer trails to walk on the Brazilian side than on the Argentinian side, I loved every bit of it!! It's simply amazing to see the biggest waterfall in the world from the front.

Should I bring food?

There are many options to buy food or drinks and so it's not really necessary to bring anything. However, there are touristy prices and it's cheaper to bring snacks from the supermarket.

How to get back into town

To get back you just take bus 120 again from the right side to the entrance for 3.75 BRL.

Other activities in Foz do Iguacu

You could visit the bird park (www.parquedasaves.com.br), a wax museum (www.dreamland.com.br/c/foz-do-igua-u/) or the three borders monument. However, everything is clearly made for the tourists and not something natural like the Iguazu Falls. Hence, I wasn't a big fan.

Some people also go on a one-day shopping trip to Paraguay. Be warned that it will be crowded with people. The Brazilian girl who stayed in my dorm didn't like her experience but if you are a shopping queen, this might be something you like.

What many people do enjoy is the Buddhist temple (Rua Dr. Josivalter Vila Nova, 99 - Foz do Iguaçu/PR). Take bus 103 to get there.

How to visit the Argentinian side of the falls from Foz do Iguacu (Brazil)

You have the option of an organized tour which you can book in town or at the hotel. The transport costs you 75 BRL and on top of that, you pay the normal entrance fee of 700 pesos (pesos or credit card). You will leave at about 8.30 a.m. and board the bus again at 5 p.m. If you want to go on the adventure boat (cost: 2000 pesos, duration: 2 hours) you should take this option as it's a bit stressful to fit in the boat if you use public transport.

How to get to Argentina by public bus

Just outside the main bus terminal (top end toward the supermarket, not the Paraguay stop), you find the Brazil-Argentina bus stop. The first bus starts at 7.25 a.m. and it's

43

either *Easy Bus* or *Rio Uruguay*. They have enough seats to sit down as opposed to bus 120 and it costs 8 BRL to get to the border. If you come back to Brazil on the same day you don't have to get off at the Brazilian border. In case you are leaving Brazil, you need to get your exit stamp. The bus won't wait for you there, but you can use your bus ticket to get on the next one (ask the driver to give you a ticket in case you haven't received one).

Then, you stamp your passport in about 2 minutes and afterward wait for the next bus from the same company which can take between 30 minutes and 1 hour. The bus then brings you to the Argentinean border (you can't walk, it's too far and too dangerous). If you stay longer than one day, you need your entry stamp. Otherwise, you stay on the bus or let the people at the counter know that you only visit for one day.

After that, the bus will either bring you to the main bus terminal of *Puerto Iguacu* (from where you take a bus to the park entrance for 20 BRL) or it will drop you somewhere along the road where you can take a shared taxi (they will ask for more than 20 BRL per person but perhaps you can haggle it down).

I didn't see any money exchange places but I didn't need pesos as I brought food and water from Brazil and the bus and taxi you could pay with small Brazilian bills.

Best way to visit Iguazu falls in Argentina

The entrance fee was 700 pesos (but with the inflation, it could change quickly) and you can pay in pesos or by credit card.

After the ticket gate, you should walk straight to the train station and get your free ticket to bring you to Devil's Throat. The trains only leave every 15 to 30 minutes and so it's best to directly get one in the morning.

In 30 minutes, you ride to the last stop. Up there are restrooms and another booth to book tours on the adventure boat. Here, the queue is shorter than at the entrance and you can book a boat tour for the afternoon. From this point on you will need at least 4 hours to see everything and if you walk all the paths you will walk about 6 km.

Walk the bridge to reach the top of a huge wall of water. Here, a raincoat might be good or otherwise, you could end up soaked.
Enjoy the spray and the colorful butterflies. You might also spot birds, turtles and big fish along the way.
After returning to the train tracks, get your free train ticket to go back to the other two paths.

The *upper circuit* is nice because you are on top of the waterfalls for the most time.
However, I really loved the *lower circuit* as you are below, next to, in front of and on top of waterfalls! If you want to know my opinion: I liked this path and the Brazilian side the best. So, you still should visit both sides ☺

If you now still have the energy for a boat ride, you can go and enjoy getting soaking wet. Otherwise, you take Rio Uruguay bus back into *Puerto Iguazu* for 180 pesos / 20 BRL, where you could spend the night or take another Rio Uruguay bus for 8 BRL back to *Foz do Iguacu* in Brazil. In case you by accident got an exit stamp before, or this is your first entry into Brazil, you now need an entry stamp again and have to wait for the bus on the Argentinian side and then on the Brazilian side. If you don't need stamps, you just ride all the way into town. 56 BRL in total for round trip transport. This isn't a big difference to the organized van and to safe yourself any stress it's probably worth it to reserve a spot on a van in your accommodation or at a travel agency.

Salvador

Salvador has two faces. On the one hand, it offers inviting beaches all around the big city and in the center, we find colorful and historic colonial-style houses. On the other hand, many houses look as if they'd fall apart any minute and because everything is built so close to each other that would end up in a huge disaster.

Anyway, if you come up to this corner of Brazil it's worth it to discover the old history of the city on one day and enjoy the beaches (perhaps even surf?) on the next day.

From the airport to the city center

The touristic centers are Barra and Pelourinho, but you will soon realize that hotels are strewn all over the place. I would say, any place along the beach is a good place to stay and with Uber or the public buses you can easily get anywhere. These are also the two means of transport to get from the airport to your hotel. With Google Maps, you can figure out, which public bus to take. They cost 4 BRL per trip. I felt safe on the buses, however, I wouldn't recommend traveling on them with big bags, since space is very limited. Uber is fairly cheap and at the airport, you can follow the Uber signs to the correct exit. A ride into town will cost between 30 and 80 BRL, depending on where you stay.

There is Wi-Fi at the airport but it's not very strong. Therefore, it's best to install the Uber app at home already.

8 things to do in Salvador

There are several neighborhoods in Salvador and if you want to visit a lot in a short time, it's best and safest to travel with Uber or buses between places.

1. Marvel at the colorful houses in Lago do Pelourinho

Quickly, you will realize that Salvador is built on hills and you will need your leg muscles to walk up and down alleys on the cobblestone roads. However, that only adds to the charm of the alleys with the many colorful houses.

2. Ride the Lacerda elevator

From the top of the terrace, you have a nice view of the marina. From the bottom, the bridge and the elevator look impressive. However, the 70m ride itself is unspectacular as it's a simple, enclosed cabin and you don't see the height. Each way is 15 Brazilian cents.

3. Ride a cable car

The more interesting way to overcome the hill from lower to upper Salvador is by funicular. There are several along the cliff. One, for example, starts from the *House of Carnival* (read number 6).

4. Relax at the beach

Barra is the most famous one. It's good for bathing as the bay is protected by rocks and the waves aren't as wild as at some other beaches around Salvador. Plus, the lighthouse offers nice picture opportunities. Apart from Barra, you have a huge choice of different beaches and you could spend weeks exploring all of them.

5. Get a massage by the beach

At Praia Jardim de Alah there is a nice grassy patch with palm trees under which you can enjoy a massage for 70 BRL / hour with the sound of the ocean in your ears. There also is a good jogging/walking path along the water and in case you get thirsty you could buy a coconut for 2 BRL.

6. Visit the House of Carnival

This is an awesome museum about the biggest party of the year. Look at colorful costumes and glitter and learn about this tradition. It's the first museum of this kind in Brazil.
Address: Praca Ramos de Queiro, s/n | Pelourinho, Salvador, Entrance fee: 30 BRL

7. Visit Convento de Sao Francisco

The interior of this church is beautiful and if you debated about which of the many churches in Salvador you should enter, this is the one to go to. There are a lot of ornaments in gold.

8. Go shopping

In case you have seen enough of the old town or it's too hot or raining cats and dogs, go to one of the modern shopping malls. *Shopping da Bahia* and *Shopping Barra* are good choices.

Lençóis and Chapada Diamantina

Lençóis is the gateway to an amazing national park with stunning canyons and waterfalls. Be aware that there are two Lençóis. The other one is at the ocean and has incredible sand dunes.

The city of Lençóis itself is more like a village. With the colorful buildings and the cobblestone roads, it's extremely charming. Plus, it's safe! Even after dark, I walked through narrow laneways on my own since the owner of my hostel told me that it's okay. You will feel this atmosphere from the first moment when you walk away from the bus station and breathe in the clean air.

How to get to Lençóis

From Salvador, there are 3 daily buses with Rapido Federal. At 7 a.m., 1 p.m. and 11 p.m. The journey takes about 7 hours and costs 90 BRL. You can buy the ticket at the terminal or online on a website like Clickbus (https://www.clickbus.com.br/). Since the buses are often fully booked, it might be a good idea to buy the ticket beforehand. In case you buy the ticket online, you have to present your ticket number at the booth of Rapido Federal at the main bus station in Salvador. You then also have to pay a terminal fee of 2 BRL.

What to do in Lençóis

Now, let's have a look at the wonders of Chapada Diamantina. Most sights involve a lot of driving and therefore are best visited on a tour with a guide. Each full-day tour costs about 200 BRL and can easily be arranged once you are in Lençóis. I booked my tours at the *Hi Hostel Chapada* and was very happy with the trips. However, you can also book arranged packages in Salvador or even online. This, of course, will turn out more expensive.

Visit Mosquito Waterfall

This waterfall is quite high and therefore impressive. Plus, the way it falls over the rocks it's spread into a nice spray. The easy walk from the car park 100m down to the river in a picturesque gorge takes 20 - 30 minutes.

Swim in Poço Azul

This is like a cenote in Mexico. You descend about 40m into a cave where you find a pool of stunningly blue water. It looks especially nice when the sun shines and different hues of blue dance in the water. Although the pool is 4-21 meters deep, and like I said, in a semi-dark cave, you can see to the ground since the water is so clear.

On the path to the cave, look out for small circles on the ground that appear as if a big raindrop had fallen there. You could open them up since they are the homes of trap-door spiders (argh, gross!).

Visit a cave

There are several caves in this area. On our tour, we visited "Gruta da Fumaca". That was an interesting experience as there are many different stalagmites and stalactites. Plus, it's not decorated like in Asian caves but left in the natural state. If you aren't claustrophobic you will enjoy crawling through the smaller sections of the cave 40m underground.

Next to "Gruta da Fumaca" was a restaurant that served a buffet lunch for 30 BRL. The food was very good and offered all the Brazilian specialties (and a lot of vegetables and salads).

Visit Fazenda Pratinha

The lagoon with its clear blue water looks very nice from further away. However, be aware that this place is a tourist trap. You can do zip-lining, snorkeling, and horseback riding. All at an additional cost. Plus, there are so many people there that it's one loud amusement park.

Enjoy the stunning view at Pai Ignacio

Now, this is the must-do stop in this area. Hike up the 150m to reach a platform. The walk from the car park takes about 20 minutes. At the top, you have a spectacular view of the valley. Be there at sunset to watch the scenery change and best come with a tour guide who vividly tells you the story of how Father Ignacio saved his people by jumping down a small ledge with an umbrella.

Bring a sweater or rain jacket as the top of the rock is completely exposed and everyone was quite cold.

The following things can easily be done on your own with maps.me:

Bathe in the Serrano swimming holes

These rock pools are only a 20-minutes' walk from the center of Lençóis. It's a fun place and we saw several people having a picnic or even a BBQ. However, it's an extremely slippery surface and you should be very careful. I met numerous people who twisted their foot while walking on the rocks. Therefore, if you want to continue to Cachoeira da Primavera afterward, I recommend that you go back on the normal path on the left side of the river and don't try to find your way on the right side of the river with maps.me. If you do continue on the right, you later will have to do a river crossing to get to the waterfalls. There is no bridge and you have to climb or jump across slippery rocks. During my stay, it rained a lot and perhaps, therefore the water level was higher. In any case, it was a dangerous adventure and not necessarily worth the risk.

Take a bath at the waterfall before Cachoeira da Primavera

This waterfall is located 30-minutes from town and an easy walk if you follow the trail along the left side of the river. The waterfall, which doesn't have a name on maps.me is also much nicer than Cachoeira da Primavera 40 minutes up the hill, which I wouldn't recommend visiting. On a nice day with a dry path, you might want to continue to Mirante viewpoint. However, you have to climb along a cliff and if you slip and fall it could be deadly. We were there on a rainy day and the climb was too difficult to really enjoy it.

About the natural waterslide

Another stroll near Lençóis brings you through the forest to Ribeirão do Meio. It might sound like a fun idea to slide down the waterfall into a river. However, it's not comfortable and you can't see below the dark water in case a swirl pulls you down. Since the walk here isn't very entertaining, I wouldn't come here and rather do something else, if your time in Lençóis is limited.

Where to eat in Lençóis

At first glance, there are only touristy restaurants with elevated prices. However, at several places you can find a local PF plate for 15 BRL. If you feel like eating a good steak, I can recommend the Steak House. The ribeye was amazing.

Itacaré

This is the surfer capital of Bahia and offers many beautiful beaches. Apart from the good waves, it is a charming but very touristy town with lots of restaurants, cheap Caipirinha places and two bars with late-night music. It's very safe, too. I could walk around the city alone even after dark without a problem. Just ask the locals about trails you should avoid on your own to be on the even safer side.

How to get to Itacaré

The closest airports are Ilhéus and Salvador. Ilhéus is more expensive but closer to Itacaré. The bus from Ilhéus airport departs hourly, takes one hour and costs about 25 BRL.

From Salvador, you have the option to take a 7-hour bus to Ilhéus and then the one-hour bus to Itacaré or you take the ferry from Salvador (Terminal Marítimo De São Joaquim) to Bom Despacho. It also departs hourly from about 5 a.m. to 8 p.m. and costs 5 BRL for the 40-minutes journey. It's nice to watch the city of Salvador growing smaller and smaller from the big ferry.

The bus station on Bom Despacho is right at the ferry terminal. The 5-hour bus from there to Itacaré costs 50 BRL.

What to do in Itacaré

Enjoy the relaxed vibe, eat a healthy smoothie bowl, and pick some of the things to do out of the following ideas.

Walk to the beaches that are close by

All beaches around Itacaré are pretty to look at. Hence, it's great to simply take a stroll, then sit down at the one you like best and drink out of a cold, fresh coconut.

Praia da Concha is the beach closest to town and best suited for swimming as the bay protects the beach from waves. It's like a swimming pool and if you like SUP, that's the place to rent a board.

The four beaches on the coast to the right of Itacaré can be reached in a 10 - 30 minutes' walk. For swimming the last one is best suited as the other ones have more rocks and riptides.

Go surfing

Advanced surfers find good waves at the four small beaches and at Jeribuçaçu. You can rent a board in Itacaré for 50 BRL for 24 hours. There are no surf shops on the beaches.

A good surf spot for beginners and everyone else is Engenhoca. Just take the ROTA bus toward Itabuna for 4 BRL and tell them you want to get off at Engenhoca. The ride takes about 20 minutes and you can take the board on the bus. After getting off, continue along the road until you reach the car park (3 minutes). Then, you follow the trail through the forest (go left at all the intersections). You can't rent boards at Engenhoca.

Take a surf lesson

Of course, you could also take some surf lessons. There are many surf shops and schools in town. 3 lessons cost about 600 BRL and 5 lessons 900 BRL.

Watch the sunset

You will witness beautiful, golden sunsets at the viewpoint from Praia da Concha. Go to the left side of the beach where all the people are and find a good spot to sit down. Usually, there are some locals selling cheap Caipirinhas.

Walk to Prainha

This secluded beach is an hour-long hike through the jungle away from Itacaré. Hence, you will have it pretty much to yourselves. Otherwise, it wasn't any different from the smaller beaches closer to Itacaré and, therefore, only worth the visit if you want to go on a walk. My hostel advised me against going alone as there had been a few robberies. In a group, you should be fine (so were we).

Eat at ZenZala

There are two restaurants with this name. The nicer one is in the historic center along the port. You can eat from the buffet for 30 BRL per kilo (so a giant plate is about 20 BRL) and they have many Brazilian delicacies plus a lot of salads and vegetables. Plenty enough for vegetarians.
Another good place for vegetarians is Point Break at the other end of Itacaré, one of the last, small restaurants before the beaches.

Dance Forró

On Wednesdays, there is a Forró party at *Jungle Bar* starting at 10.30 p.m. The entry fee is 5 BRL and it's worth to check it out even if you don't know how to dance yet. Perhaps, someone will teach you.

Where to stay in Itacaré

I stayed at *Buddy's Hostel* which had a great atmosphere and a good breakfast. The garden with the hammocks was especially nice and you could also chill there when it rained since everything had a roof.

From Itacaré to Rio by bus

If you are up for a 24- hour bus ride instead of flying, best go to the bus station to buy your ticket. That turns out about 100 BRL cheaper than buying it online. I took the route via Ubaitaba and then a direct bus ride to Rio with Gontijo. The journey was quite okay, except that the bus arrived 2 hours late.

The trip cost 325 BRL in total. I think you can get it cheaper, but I only bought the ticket in the same week as I traveled. Two weeks ago, flying from Salvador with GOL was the same price, however, now flights cost over 1000 BRL. So, it's best to plan your journeys ahead. On the other hand, many travelers stay in Itacaré much longer than they intended since it's so charming.

Rio de Janeiro

Rio is a vibrant and colorful city with a nice climate throughout the year. Even in July (winter here), we had a sunny 28 degrees during the day and many people from Argentina were spending their winter holiday in Rio.

The numerous different neighborhoods make it impossible to see Rio in one day. So, take your time to stroll along the nice Flamengo walk and marvel at the stunning bay with Christ the Redeemer and Sugarloaf Mountain (Pão de Açúcar), visit the sights in Lapa and drink a Caipirinha at Copacabana beach. Read the chapter about safety information before you go to Rio.

From the airport to the city center

From the international airport (GIG) to downtown the quickest and easiest way is an Uber for about 80 BRL.

If you arrive during the day you can also check on Google maps, which connection with public transport works out the quickest to get to your accommodation. I traveled on buses, the metro, and the tram during daylight hours and felt safe.

Go to the BRT station at the airport and make the connection to Vicente de Carvalho metro station. From there, you can ride the metro trains and switch onto other lines until you reach the desired destination. You need a *RioCard* to enter the trams and buses. It costs 5 BRL and you have to top it up with money. When you get it, you can also get a map of the metro and tram system and check for the current prices. It depends on which kind of transport you ride and whether you combine several methods of transportation of how much it will cost. A ride on a bus usually costs 4.05 BRL, a tram ride costs 3.80 BRL and a ride with the metro 4.65 BRL.

If this sounds too complicated you can catch the official airport bus that leaves from outside Terminal 2 and stops in the Center, Gloria, Catete, Largo do Machado, Flamengo, Botafogo, Copacabana, Ipanema, Leblon, and Barra da Tijuca, and costs 16 BRL.

Arriving at Novo Rio Bus station

Outside the bus station, you can also catch buses or trams into the downtown area where you can switch onto a Metro, which is quicker. The buses can be paid in cash to the driver as well.

What to do in Rio

Even the locals (called Cariocas) who live here all year round say that in this city, you can never get bored. Rio welcomes you with great museums, colorful neighborhoods, iconic sites, cheap Caipirinhas and all of that is set next to the glistering ocean.

Wander through Lapa and Santa Theresa

Here you find colorful buildings, stunning murals and the Escadaria Selarón (Selaron Steps) which offer great picture opportunities. But don't just get your picture and leave. Take your time to study the individual tiles. There should be one for each country.

Also, at the bottom of the stairs, you find the cheapest Caipirinha in Rio. Be careful though, they are very strong, and one glass might be enough to make you drunk! And when you are drunk, you will probably get robbed. I heard many stories of this kind.

I felt very safe on the walk around Lapa as there were many other tourists around us taking pictures as well. But in case you want a more guided experience, join a well-done free walking tour (www.freetour.com/rio-de-janeiro/lapa-and-downtown) which starts at 10.30 a.m. every day at Carioca Square.

Visit Christ the Redeemer (El Cristo Redentor)

From many spots in Rio, you will see this statue watching over the city on clear days. It's possible to hike up to the entrance to the statue. For that, take the bus to Parque Lage and then ask for the hike to Christ the Redeemer (caminhada para Cristo el Redentor). It's steep, humid, and will take you about 1.5 to 2 hours. Plus, it's along a busy road and you have to avoid the vans that come and go. Hence, it's neither a nice nor a safe walk. At the top, you have to buy the entrance ticket for 22 BRL.

We chose the van as a transport option from Largo do Machado. Apparently, it was low season in April as we had to wait for other people to arrive and fill up the van. However, I heard that in high season, the lines are very long. You can also board a van at Lido Square in Copacabana and at Barra da Tijuca outside Citta America Shopping Center. We paid 51 BRL at the counter. In high season it would cost 62 BRL. You can also purchase the tickets online (www.paineirascorcovado.com.br/viva-a-experiencia#embarque) and skip the lines in case it's busy. They brought us to a first viewing platform with a climatized van. There, you switch onto a different van which brings you to the impressive statue. You can stay up there as long as you like. Take in the view of the many white buildings in front of the blue sea and the green hills. There also is a café in case you are hungry or thirsty.

Enjoy the view from Sugarloaf Mountain

This is the most iconic landmark of Rio apart from Christ the Redeemer. You can take a modern cable car up to a viewing platform. The cheapest ticket costs 104 BRL and is best bought online (www.bondinho.com.br/en/home/#ingressos) as you will have a 10% discount. Check on Google Maps how to get to Bondinho Pão de Açúcar (Av. Pasteur, 520 – Urca) with public transport or on foot. If the cable car is too expensive for you, there apparently is a path you can hike, however, it really is not advisable to walk up there regarding safety. Perhaps, you enjoy it more to look at the mountain from the boardwalk along the beaches or from the viewing platform at El Cristo anyway.

Stroll along Flamengo Walk

This walk leads through green parks and along the beaches of Flamengo, Botafogo, and Gloria. You will encounter many cyclists and runners and could buy a fresh coconut from one of the street vendors. Here you forget that you are in a big city.

Eat at Fogo de Chao

This restaurant is at the start (or end) of the Flamengo walk in Botafogo. It's a chain churrascaria restaurant which you can also find in Sao Paulo. Their buffet is huge and offers a big choice of healthy and delicious salads. If you only eat from the buffet without the hot meat it costs 60 BRL. This, of course, is more expensive than other restaurants, but you have to see the buffet! There even is salmon, ceviche, salami, bacon, cheese, and antipasti apart from all the salads. Hence, it's possible to have a great meal there without ordering the steaks or chicken. There is plenty of delicious food without it. Plus, this restaurant is set right in the bay and has a terrace overlooking the boats, sea, and Sugarloaf Mountain.

Visit a museum

The three best museums in Rio are the Museum of Tomorrow, the Rio Art Museum and the Modern Art Museum.

- The **Museum of Tomorrow** is an impressive building designed by the famous architect Santiago Calatrava. The whole area is worth to take a stroll around. Along the tram tracks, you see huge graffiti by famous Brazilian artist Kobra (this is free). The science museum itself offers a great, interactive exhibition about what challenges we are facing in the future, regarding sustainability. The entrance fee is 20 BRL. It is closed on Mondays. (https://museudoamanha.org.br/en)

- The **Art Museum of Rio** is right opposite the Museum of Tomorrow and you can look at paintings from famous artists from all around the world. The entrance fee is 20 BRL and it's free on Tuesdays! If you visit both the Museu de Arte and the Museu do Amanhã the combined ticket costs 32 BRL.
(https://museudeartedorio.org.br/en/visit-us/time-and-tickets/)

- The **Museum of Modern Art** is located in a park (Av Infante Dom Henrique 85, Parque do Flamengo) where many locals gather to do sports like rollerblading, yoga or dancing. Hence, it's an entertaining area even if you don't enter the museum as modern art might not be the taste of everyone. The admission is 14 BRL and it's free on Wednesdays.
(https://www.mam.rio/visitacao/)

Get perfect Instagram photos

Where? In a library. Yes, Rio might have the most beautiful room full of books in the world. It's called the Royal Portuguese Reading Room (Real Gabinete Português da Leitura). It's free to enter, you just have to sign in at the entrance. The address is R. Luís de Camões, 30 - Centro, Rio de Janeiro.

Surf at Copacabana or Ipanema Beach

First of all, I have never seen such crowded beaches. Not even Kuta on Bali. Therefore, it's not a very relaxing beach stay but people clearly enjoy hanging out on the sand and playing around in the waves. Vendors will bring you food or drinks and the view on the hills at the end of the beach is quite unique.

Be warned that anything you bring to the beaches of Copacabana or Ipanema might get stolen. Don't wear a necklace or they will rip it off (heard that this happened to several girls I met) or even if they were laying next to their backpack and had their foot on it, they sometimes got stolen. Therefore, only leave your stuff at the beach if you are in a group and bring it in a plastic bag (not in a backpack). Best don't take your phone with you. If you only come for a walk and don't sit down on the sand, you should be fine with taking pictures. I saw other people with their big cameras, and I took pictures while I was on a walk as well and I am still in possession of all my belongings.

If you want to do sports, you can rent a surfboard or boogie board for 40 BRL per hour. Good waves for advanced surfers were on the left side of Ipanema near the rocks. However, there were so many people in each other's way that it wasn't enjoyable at all. I liked the spot in the middle of Copacabana much better, where smaller waves rolled in consistently, and the people could spread out a bit more.

Surfing near Rio

45 min South by bus you reach **Recreio dos Bandeirantes**. I stayed there for one week at one of the surf camps and really enjoyed the waves. I took a lesson the first day but just went in on my own after that since it was very safe.

The nice thing is that you can see the white buildings of Rio up north, but it doesn't feel like big city life down here at all. You can easily explore more beaches by riding the bicycle along the cycling path and even after dark the area is safe to walk around and find a good place to have dinner.

Ilha Grande

This is said to be the nicest island between Rio and Sao Paulo and I very much enjoyed the clear waters with view on some other, smaller, green islands. Plus, it's a nice change of pace as there are no cars on Ilha Grande. Near the port there are hostels, pousadas, restaurants, and some paved roads but otherwise, it's all sand and jungle paths.

How to get to Ilha Grande

From Rio, take a *Costa Verde* bus to Conceição de Jacareí. This is the town that is located closest to Ilha Grande. A boat trip from here only takes 20 to 30 minutes and costs 20 to 30 BRL. The bus trip takes 2.5 hours and costs around 58 BRL. Buses leave all day and boats leave between 6.30 a.m. and 6 p.m. The port on Ilha Grande is called Abraão.

From Sao Paulo, take a bus by *Reunidas* to Angra dos Reis. The trip takes about 7.5 hours and costs 35 USD. At the bus stop in Angra dos Reis, you find ticket agencies from boat offices who want to take you to Ilha Grande. Depending on which boat you get, the trip to Abraão will take one or two hours and will cost 40 BRL or 13 BRL.

What to do on Ilha Grande

On Ilha Grande, everything is still small and personal. Family-run pousadas and local restaurants. Therefore, it's a great place to disconnect from the rest of the world a little and simply relax at one of the beaches or attempt a hike through the jungle.

Visit the most beautiful beach in Brazil

Lopes Mendes beach is said to be the most beautiful beach in Brazil. It's a long stretch of white sand, wild, blue water and foam on the waves. It's not the most beautiful beach I've ever been at but it's certainly worth a trip while on Ilha Grande.

To get to Lopes Mendes you can take a boat from the pier in Abraão. They start leaving at 9.30 a.m. A round trip ticket costs 30 BRL but you can also just buy one way and then hike the way back through the jungle. We did that and it took us about three hours. It's a straining hike up and down slippery hills (and this in the Brazilian heat), past smaller beaches and across flooded bays. So, bring enough water and shoes you feel comfortable to walk in.

The boat from Abraão can't actually bring you to Lopes Mendes beach but drops you off at a smaller beach on the other side of a hill. The hike across the hill takes about 20 minutes. At Lopes Mendes, there is no infrastructure except for a few locals who might sell you a beer. Therefore, bring everything you need for a day at the beach. Check at what time the last boat back to Abraão leaves.

If it hasn't just rained heavily, this is a nice hike as well and you can enjoy taking a shower at the 15m high waterfall in the end. The trail to Cachoeira da Feiticeira starts on the right side of the island if you face the island from the pier. You will pass another waterfall with a pond, where you can also swim. After that, the trail gets quite difficult and it will still take an hour from that point.

Find your private beach

Simply hike along the shore and find yourself a quiet spot of beach between the palm trees. Who said that you have to settle where other tourists are already?

Have dinner on the beach

In the evening, the restaurants set out candles and often there is a guitar player who adds an even more romantic feeling. Try the seafood Moqueca.
If the food at the beach is too expensive for you, walk along the road behind the church. There, you find the cheapest restaurants and Caipirinha bars.

Where to stay on Ilha Grande

Che Lagarto is located at one end of the beach and has a nice terrace as a perfect location for sunset drinks. It's a social hostel in which you can meet new friends quickly.

TIPP: Bring enough cash. There are no ATMs on Ilha Grande and often, there is no connection to the credit card machines.
Also, there are no roads or taxis, so you might think twice about carrying a heavy suitcase across the sand. Perhaps, this still rather is a place for backpackers?

Paraty

This is a very picturesque colonial town by the sea with the possibility to do some boat trips to islands and waterfalls. If you haven't been to any nice beaches, you might do a boat tour here and if you haven't seen other colonial towns in Brazil, Paraty is worth exploring. It's great to simply stroll around the colorful buildings with your camera in hand and browse through the art shops. However, if you don't do a tour to the waterfalls, you will have seen Paraty in half a day.

How to get to Paraty

From Rio: Catch a Costa Verde bus from Novo Rio bus station. The trip takes 4.5 hours and costs about 20 USD.

From Ilha Grande: Take a ferry to the mainland (for example to Angra do Reis) and from there you catch a local *Colitur* bus along the main road. It takes about 1 hour and 45 minutes and costs around 17 BRL.

From Sao Paulo: Take a bus (Reunidas) from the main bus terminal. The journey takes about 6 hours and costs around 27 USD.

Sao Paulo

Sampa, as the locals call this big city, is a place you will only get a small glimpse of as a tourist. It consists of many different neighborhoods that are best reached by metro, bus or Uber. Sampa doesn't have a beach like Rio but it offers a lot of cultural entertainment and modern shopping malls.

How to get from the airport or bus station to the city center

Both times I came to Sao Paulo I used the public bus to get to and from the airport, even though it was after dark. I stayed in Vila Madalena, near the metro station, which is a safe area to walk around with your luggage. Perhaps in the Paulista area, it's safer to just take an Uber.

By public bus from Guarulhos: From Guarulhos airport, board bus 257 to Tatuapê metro station (red line). It departs from terminal 3 and takes about 1 hour, depending on traffic. It costs 6.45 BRL and has to be paid in cash. From Tatuapê, you take an Uber to your accommodation or go on by metro to the closest station to your hostel. A ride on the metro (Bilhete Unico) costs 3.50 BRL.

From Congonhas Airport: Several buses run from this airport to the downtown area. Ask a local which bus you should take to your hostel or check on Google maps. A trip costs 4.30 BRL and takes half an hour to an hour. The closest metro station is São Judas (blue line). Take bus 609 from outside the arrivals hall to get to the metro station. A combined bus and metro ticket will cost you 7.50 BRL.

From the Terminal Rodoviário Tietê (main bus terminal): Conveniently, the terminal is also connected to a metro station (Tietê) on the blue line. Hence, board a train that goes toward Jabaquara and switch onto another train which brings you to the station you need or get off directly at the station closest to your hotel.

What to do in Sao Paulo

Sao Paulo is an awesome city to live in as there is always something going on. As a tourist, you won't be able to visit everything, but it has something to offer for everyone.

Shop at Rua 25 de Março

In this busy street which feels like everyday carnival, you find the cheapest prices in Brazil for clothing, accessories, phone items, etc. It's located right in front of the central market (Mercado Municipal).

Taste fruit and buy seafood at the Mercado Municipal

This is a big food market where you can eat the famous, huge pastrami sandwich. The good thing about the market is that they will offer you all kinds of fruit to try for free. This way, you can get to know all the flavors of South American fruits without spending a cent. For future breakfasts and snacks, you now also know which fruit to buy in case you are craving something healthy.

In the seafood section at the booth in the right corner, you can buy fresh sashimi for very cheap. Usually, they only serve it on Saturdays at the shop in front of the ATMs but if you ask nicely, you can buy it at the counter in the corner every day and then get to eat it at their other booth in front of the ATMs (or take it home).

The restaurant in the center of the seafood market is great for Oysters and beer.

Visit a museum

Sao Paulo has a huge variety of cultural places to offer and if you are there on the right day, you can even enjoy them for free. The following are my favorites.

- **The Pinacoteca**

This was my favorite art museum in Sao Paulo as it is a nice building (worth the visit itself) and had an awesome exhibition when I was there. It normally costs 10 BRL but is free on Saturdays. It is located in front of the Luz metro station. (http://pinacoteca.org.br/en/)

- **The Sao Paulo Museum of Art (MASP)**

This art museum contains works of art from artists from all around the world. You can't miss the big, red building when you walk along Paulista Avenue (MASP or Trianon metro station). It normally costs 30 BRL but is free on Tuesdays.

At first, I was a bit shocked about how they display the paintings. Instead of neatly being hung on walls in different rooms, they were all lined up in rows in a huge, loft-like hall. However, after wandering through a few rows, I became a big fan of this installation as it lets you view the work from all sides, and you can get really close to the paintings. (https://masp.org.br/en)

- **The Football Museum**

If you like soccer, you might like this museum (Praça Charles Miler, s/n - Pacaembu, São Paulo). Unfortunately, there were no displays or videos in English and so I walked through it rather quickly. The cool thing is that you can go inside the big football stadium of Sao Paulo, which is quite impressive. It costs 20 BRL but is free on Tuesdays. (www.museudofutebol.org.br/pagina/horarios-e-ingressos)

Shop or drink coffee at Paulista Avenue

You probably can't go to Sao Paulo without spending time at Paulista Avenue. Along the avenue, you find shopping malls with all the well-known shops and restaurants.

Go see a movie

In case it rains or is very hot you might want to seek shelter at a movie theater. Just make sure the movie is in English if you can't speak Portuguese. I watched a 3d movie at the IMAX on Paulista Avenue and it only cost 18.50 BRL including the glasses.

Dive into Japanese culture

There are Japanese restaurants all over Sao Paulo. In fact, Sao Paulo has the biggest Japanese community living outside Japan. Go to the area called Liberdade. It feels a bit as if you landed in a different country.

Discover Graffiti

Sao Paulo is a city of treasures regarding colorful and skillful graffiti. The most famous location is Batman Alley which you can find on your own with maps.me. However, if you have time, I recommend that you do a free walking tour of Vila Madalena*. The local guides will tell you the stories behind the graffiti and you get to see more graffiti than just Beco do Batman. In the end, you pay a donation of as much as you think the tour was worth. The pace of the tour was a bit slow for my taste but the graffiti we saw were amazing.

*https://www.saopaulofreewalkingtour.com/

Where to stay

Vila Magdalena was a safe neighborhood the two times I stayed there, and it was no problem walking around on my own after dark. Near Paulista and other places it's a different story. I talked to a local and a volunteer and they had both been robbed in Sao Paulo. The local and her mother were even held at gunpoint and 5 out of 8 volunteers were robbed during their stay. So, read the safety advice before coming to Sao Paulo and I hope you have such a good and safe experience in Sampa as I did.

I loved **Hostel Alice** in Vila Madalena. It's 2 minutes from the metro station and apart from having a vegan bakery, they also have a garden with hammocks, a TV with a Netflix account and they offer free yoga or meditation classes in the evening! I wished I could have stayed longer.

Lençóis Maranhenses

This is probably one of the most unique places in the world and pictures of it look absolutely spectacular! Unfortunately, I haven't made it there yet as it is quite far away from the other cities mentioned in this guide and I didn't want to book two more flights just to visit Lençóis Maranhenses. But because it's so amazing and you might want to visit it, I include the description my friend gave me.

Lençóis Maranhenses is an area with dunes that are filled with lagoons that consist of rainwater. So, it looks like a desert but it's not. In order that there is water between the dunes, the beauty of this place slightly depends on the rainy season and the best months to visit are July and August (that's when my friend went). May, June, and September are also possible.

How to get there: Fly to Sao Luis. Then, book a bus to Barreirinhas. You can book it directly at the airport or at any hotel and it takes 4 to 5 hours.
Once in Barreirinhas, you book your desired tour. The tours usually involve several lagoons. You will be shuttled around the dunes in 4x4 vehicles and on car ferries.

Amazon – Manaus

The gateway to the Brazilian Amazon is the city of Manaus. Manaus has a rather interesting story as it used to be one of the richest cities in the world when the world needed natural rubber. Therefore, you can find a glamorous theater in the center of town as a reminder of the good old times. Unfortunately, they didn't innovate their product as artificial rubber was invented and soon business had gone stale and the rich society left Manaus.

The former heyday of Manaus is difficult to imagine today when walking through the town. Especially after dark, you should not necessarily walk around alone. It's best if you find a tour that you feel comfortable with as soon as possible or take the boat to other well-known places along the Amazon.

How to get there

Manaus has an airport and therefore you can check whether direct flights are available. Probably, it will be cheaper to first book an international flight to Sao Paulo, Rio or Fortaleza (the biggest airport in northern Brazil).
From the airport, a taxi to the center costs around 55 BRL. You can take bus 306 for 3.80 BRL. Ask whether it goes to the center.

Traveling to Manaus by bus is not recommended as it will take you several days and the bus runs through non-touristy areas.

A boat trip on the Amazon

Many people go to the Amazon to experience the river on a boat. For example, you could take a five-day boat trip from Belem (quicker from Manaus to Belem as it's downstream). You will have to bring your own hammock and rope in which you will sleep. The ticket for the trip costs about 200 BRL. You can buy food on board and the taste is fine, but many foreigners seem to get stomach problems, which is not so great if everyone is using the same, tiny boat toilets. So, you might have an enjoyable trip if you can bring cooking gear and food. Or, at least eat your own food on the first day and see how other tourists are reacting.

Also, apparently, cabins don't cost much more than hammocks but then again, sleeping in a hammock on a boat is quite a cool experience. Since it rains a lot in the rain forest it is useful to bring plastic bags in which you can keep your luggage.

If you want to go from Manaus to **Colombia** you can catch a daily fast boat (36 hours in a seat, bring blankets and warm clothes for the a/c) for about 600 BRL to Tabatinga (city next to Leticia). Three daily meals are included, and I've heard good things about the food. Once you arrive in Leticia, don't forget to get your exit stamp from Brazil and the entry stamp toa Colombia or you might have a problem later. In case you have troubles to get the stamps, catch a taxi to the airport in Leticia and do immigration there.

The slow boat to Leticia takes 7 days (it's faster from Tabatinga to Manaus as it's downstream). It leaves on Saturday and Wednesday. If you sleep in your own hammock it will cost you around 350 BRL with three daily meals. A cabin with a private bathroom is around 800 BRL for two people and perhaps worth it for such a long journey.

From Tabatinga you can also travel onwards to Iquitos in **Peru**. There are two boat companies which do the 10-hour boat ride (the price is about 70 USD). Check the websites of *Transporte Goflhino* and *Transtur S.A.* You can write them an e-mail with your questions.

Things to do in Manaus

Apart from touring the glamorous theater, you could visit the **Meeting of the Waters**. Two different rivers are flowing into each other which creates an interesting color mix. It's best to be observed from the air and perhaps you are lucky to spot it when you fly in. Then, there are tours or multi-day cruises to **spot wildlife**. You will be able to book a tour from the offices in Manaus and can find a tour you feel comfortable with.

In case you do travel to the Amazon, remember that it's the lungs of our planet and we need it. So, in case you find a project that protects the Amazon, it will be worth it to support such projects as a tourist.

Did you like this travel guide?

In case you liked this travel guide, I'd greatly appreciate a positive review on Amazon, and it would be a good support if you told your friends about it ☺

Some useful words in Portuguese

English	Portuguese
Hello	Olá / Bom dia!
Everything ok? (Used like: How are you?)	Tudo bem?
I'm well and you?	Bem, e você?
Where are you from?	De onde você é?
I'm from…	Eu sou de..(Estados Unidos, Inglaterra)
Yes	Sim
No	Não
Please, write it down.	Por favor, escreva.
Where is the toilet?	Onde está o banheiro?
Thank you.	Obrigado (if you are male)/ obrigada (female)
How much is…?	Quanto custa....?
Sorry	desculpa
please	por favor
I need to change money.	Preciso trocar dinheiro
I would like…	Eu quero…
Water	Água
Chicken	Frango
Without meat	Sem carne
What time does… arrive?	Que horas chega…?
Plane	Avião
Boat	Barco
Waterfall	Cachoeira
Right	Direita
Left	Esquerda
Straight ahead	Reto

Do you need more info?

In case you need more info, I am happy to help. Contact or follow me through these channels:

(b) www.swissmissontour.com

(i) @swissmissontour

(f) SwissMissOnTour

(w) www.slgigerbooks.wordpress.com

By the way, since the photos in this travel guide are black and white, you can send me an e-mail and I will send you the e-book version of I love Brazil for free. In the e-book, the pictures are in color.

More books by S. L. Giger

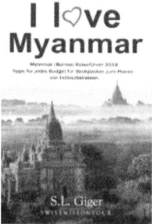

Made in United States
Orlando, FL
01 February 2023

29342498R00055